Yo

June 9, 2018
Hip Hop Ed Conference
Teachers College, Columbia University
New York City, New York
United States of America

Rediscovering an ancient
script through Hip Hop
Kristian Kabuay
BAYBAY SCHOOL

"It's like a jungle sometimes, it makes me wonder how I keep from going under." Imagine the writing system that this classic line from Melle Mel disappearing off the face of the Earth forever.

It's like a jungle sometimes
It makes me wonder how I keep from goin' under

I, like many immigrants, have the traditional common narrative of a vicious dictator in a third world country backed by Americans, and the folks from my country moved to a colonial power. I have that story.

Sunday Express

10 centavos

FM DECLARES MARTIAL LAW

The nat'l situation in brief

But civilian gov't still functions; no military takeover

To save the Republic and form a new society

Nation is calm; business, life go on normally

As a kid, my family migrated over to America from the Philippines to escape this dictator. And it was a typical story, hustle, immigrants, parents come over, want their kids to live a better life. I remember I was in second grade and this kid walked up to me, he goes, "What are you?" I go, "I'm American," he goes, "No, you're not," I didn't have a comeback. So, I go home, talked to my mom, and say, "Mom, this kid in school said I'm not American," "You're not, you're Filipino." Oh, alright, I didn't know what that was. I go back to that kid, tap him on the shoulder, look up (he was taller than me), say, "Hey," "What?" "I'm Filipino," he goes, "What's that?" I had no come back again. That was like my first lesson in the dynamics of identity; second grade.

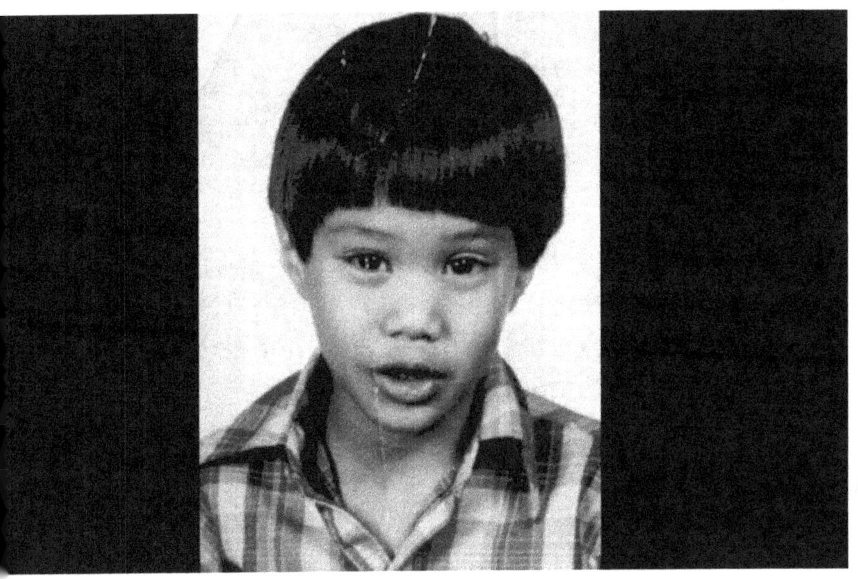

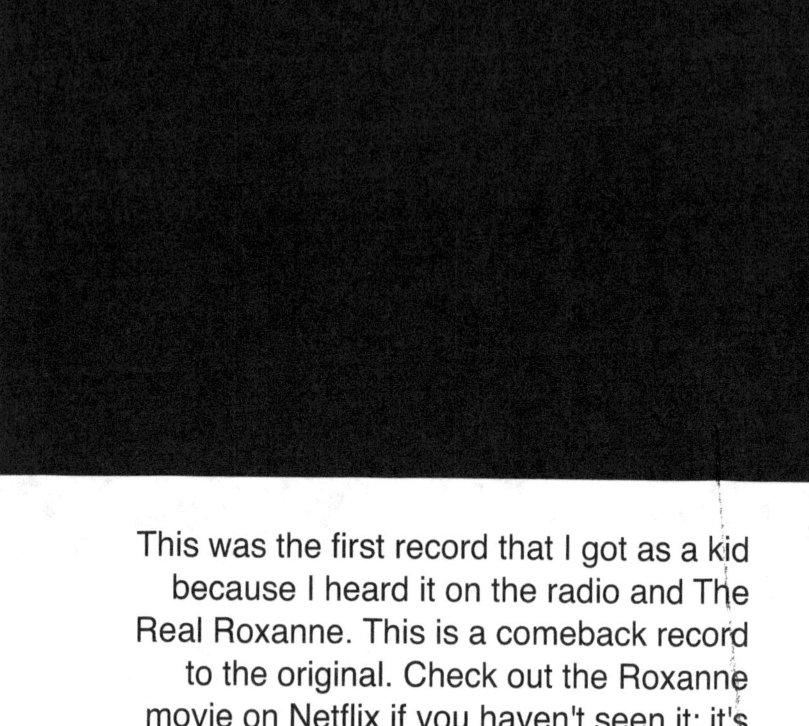

This was the first record that I got as a kid because I heard it on the radio and The Real Roxanne. This is a comeback record to the original. Check out the Roxanne movie on Netflix if you haven't seen it; it's awesome. And I remember getting this that I hear on the radio, buying the record as a little kid, it was one of the first things that I bought with my own money. And I was just thinking, "Man, I'll listen to this back and forth," and just hearing them kind of having this conversation, it was different, it was...only music that I heard was Frank Sinatra from my dad in the car, so this was really different, and I was already hooked as I started getting more into the music.

SELECT
RECORDS
ROXANNE
(with UTFO)
FMS
62256
Stereo
33 1/3
RPM
SIDE A
THE REAL ROXANNE* 4:39
(Full Force, UTFO)
Produced & Arranged by Full Force
Executive Producer - Fred Munao
ADRA Music/K.E.O. Music/Mokojumbi Music - BMI
© 1984 Select Records
*Bleeped Version
SELECT RECORDS 175 FIFTH AVE. NEW YORK, NEW YORK 10010

It hit me in all sense; Hip Hop did, it was obviously visually then it was audibly and then physically through break dancing. There were classic movies, I grew up watching these. I actually like Beat Street better, Breakin' was kind of corny kind of like Fame. Beat Street had Spit and was right here in New York City, I didn't know anything about New York. I learned everything about New York through Hip Hop, through movies, through Beastie Boys, through KRS-One and Nas and all of those folks. But all of this as a kid it was kind of like was so different from what I was experiencing. Usually, the narrative's moving to a city and then when your parents make good, then you move out to the burbs.

And that's when I started to practice my
practice of Hip Hop. Breakdancing that's
the physical-ness then through art.

Like most kids, everyone here started out
as an artist when your drawing. In case,
drawing ninjas and dragons and all that, all
of us started that. But eventually,
something happens that makes us stop.

WHEN WE WERE YOUNG
WE ALL WERE ARTISTS

In my case, it stopped when this happened; I got an F on my math test. And most parents, of course, they want their kids to do good, but coming from an immigrant context, like, my father, he went to like the Harvard or the Stanford of the Philippines. But when he came to America, he had to work at a hardware store even though he spoke perfect English he didn't

learn the native language until he was in high school, but he grew up speaking English. But when he came out to America, it still wasn't good enough. Even though he was smarter than everyone else, but because he had a little accent then, alright, you can't work here, so he had to work at a

hardware store. So, then that context is then is "Alright I want my kid to do better than me" We all want that, but it was too much, it was an exaggeration of what America was supposed to be, and as an immigrant kid you get that burning.

So, it was frowned upon that I draw at home. So each time I would draw dad would go, "What are you doing? Go study your math, memorize your math timetables or whatever." So, I couldn't draw at home, so what I do? Went back down to the railroad tracks and just to explore, cry, or whatever and I found -discovered this- and I've only seen it in the movies, seen some kids spray painting or old school shoe polish mops, filling it with ink and brake fluid making drips. So, immediately I said, "Damn, that's cool," fell in love with it. It kind of had that DIY where you had to make your own because they didn't... nowadays you can just go to some store and buy a graffiti pen, back then you had to make them. So, this is what I fell in love with after I couldn't draw at home. I would try and sneak some things in, but it was mainly the walls around the corner at the railroad tracks from my house.

"Mike" DREAM

I used to go with my grandfather to Chinatown I asked him, "What's that writing system?" I'd say, "Oh, that looks like graffiti," "No, that's how they write in China," I go, "Oh, how did you write when you were a kid in the Philippines?" He goes, "Oh, we wrote in English." It just seemed weird to me, I couldn't really comprehend, but it just seemed strange.

天仁茗茶
HSBC
廣
隆
天仁 茗茶
TenRen's TEA
匯生廣
N.G GIFTS

So, my next practice, I guess, was around the DIY (Do It Yourself) space and it's...you've heard the term like "Making champagne out of garbage juice." So, what I found out was that...I was reading The Source and Craig Mack he said that he didn't know anybody in the record business so in the records he looked, alright, where's Loud Records, where's Arista, and he would look them up and go up and down New York and try and find where these labels were, and he hustled. And I took that same way that he did that was, hey, maybe I could get some free records somewhere. So, I found the same record addresses, I wrote them a letter and say, "Hey, I'm going to open up a record store," I was like 12 years old, "I'm going to open a record store," sent them a letter and the next thing they sent me a packet with like orders and a bunch of free CDs. I was like, "Damn, this thing works what Craig Mack did."
(Audience laughter)

Craig Mack

Back then when I was a kid I was collecting baseball cards, basketball cards what if I do the same thing for this maybe they'll send me some free stuff. So, I did that, and then they send me some free a box of NBA cards and baseball cards, sample. They wanted me to be a distributor, and I didn't really know anything about that. So, I stole my dad's business license, made a copy of it, went to the bank, saved up all my cash and got a cashier's check and the next thing you know I'm like 12 years old, and I'm the distributor for these basketball cards. And then you know you sell them in school, and you get suspended and all of that but all, because of, what I learned from Craig Mack. (Audience laughter)

I'm from San Francisco, the bay. And in the Bay, there's...our Hip Hop is a bit different, home of E40, Too Short, MC Hammer, Souls of Mischief, Hieroglyphics crew, all of that. But one thing that not a lot of people know about the Bay is that there's a book called Legion of Boom, and it outlines the rise of Filipino American DJs within the Bay area. During the 80's when they roes everyone knew a Filipino DJ to rock a house party. All over the Bay, all cities. And some of you may know of some of the Rock Steady DJs from the legendary Rock Steady Crew. The story is that Crazy Legs saw DJ Qbert and say, "Hey, I want you guys to be my DJ," so they went on tour with him, they won DMC World Championships. The crew consisted of these guys that I knew of them, but I didn't know that they were Filipinos, DJ Qbert...do you believe that he's like 50 years old? This dude is 52 years old. DJ Qbert, Mix Master Mike who was the Dj for the Beastie Boys and DJ Apollo. So, these guys they were the ones that helped reinvent making the turntable an instrument.

E40
Too Short
MC Hammer
Souls of Mischief
Del
DJ Qbert
Mix Master Mike
DJ Apollo

My next practice then was as a DJ, but I couldn't really afford the turntables, so I played cassette tapes at school. Somehow, I convinced the principal that I can be a DJ during lunch time. (Audience laughter) And, of course, I would play this stuff, and I would beep out the bad words, things like that, but they didn't understand anyway. But I was playing Public Enemy, KRS, and throw in some Bob Marley and even some NWA, beeping out some stuff.

But what was interesting was that when I was a kid, pulling out a CD, a record, you had the liner notes, you could read the lyrics. Spotify has Rap Genius incorporated, but you can't really read the lyrics, or you look at a sample and try to dig through the crates, try and find that sample from Miles Davis or John Coltrane.

Public Enemy
KRS-One
PRT
Brand Nubian
NWA
Bob Marley

With this album, Boogie Down Productions, there was this one song that woke me up. So, it was very biblical and coming from...because my grandmother is very, very Catholic, so once a month we'd go to her house and kneel on the ground and say all the Hail Mary on the wooden floor and "Aww man, why are we doing this, my knees hurt, Sunday we're supposed to be resting." (Audience laughter) I remember hearing this, he goes, " Abraham was the father of Issac, and Issac was the father of Jacob," but this line right here, "In this era black Egyptians weren't right, they enslaved black Israelites, Moses had to be of the black race because he spent forty years in Pharaoh's place. He passed as the Pharaoh's grandson, so he had to look just like him." And I remember watching the ten commandments on TV "Moses, he's a white guy you look like Santa Claus," (Audience laughter) Oh, wait, I looked on the map, oh wait, Egypt is in Africa so why is he white? And I was young, and that really messed me up. I know sometimes KRS just rhymes just for rhyme sake, but I was thinking, "Man, it just didn't make sense to me. So, I ask my grandmother,

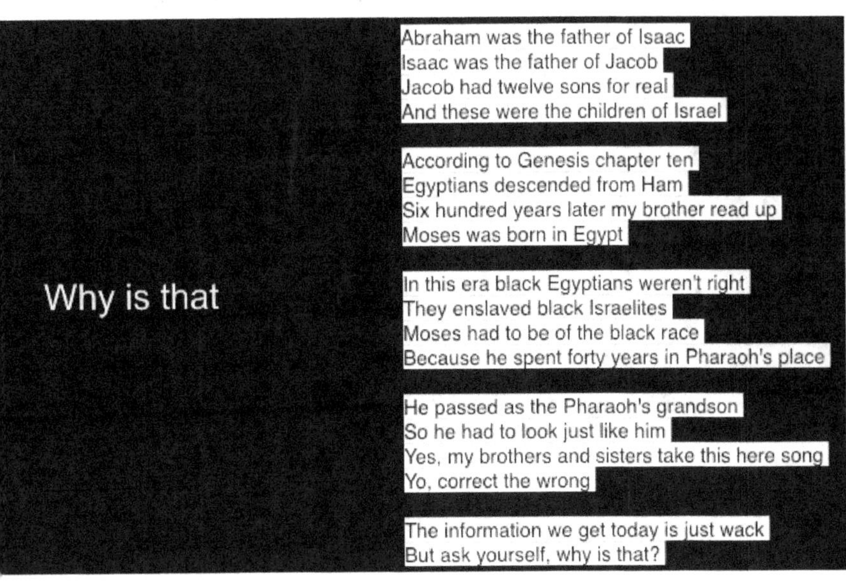

"Grandma, how come Jesus has blue eyes
and blond hair?" And started throwing all
the stuff, "That's lies, don't do that."

That lead me to learning about Malcolm X, Marcus Garvey, Black Panthers. And then I start to question who are the folks that are the revolutionaries for my people during that colonial time, I didn't really know, so that forced me to search for my own identity.

X

This happened in school, I'm sure a lot of you had to do this. The funny thing is that when I was in school I was excited about it and I went home to my grandparents, "Hey, I need to do this family tree," they said, "Alright, well who's your grandparents, grandpa, who's your grandparents?" "I don't know, they're dead, don't matter." And they couldn't really tell, it wasn't because of some shame or something as easy as there were no papers, no birth certificate. I went to school, I filled out my chart for my family tree, my classmate, his name was something like John Smith, he goes, "Boom," it was like this deep, he had all the way Duke of Norman-whatever (Audience Laughter) he, even had a picture of his ancestors. He went deep, and he was explaining, and I took my paper out, had to get my classmate to help hold it coz I had to tape it sideways. I had no tree, I had a bush with just me and all my cousins. (Audience Laughter) I could only go as deep as my grandparents because that's all I could know or maybe there's some trauma that they don't want to talk about. So, I just had all my aunts, uncles and my cousins, so I had my family bush.

That moment when the teacher asks you for a family tree...
AND YOU'RE FILIPINO

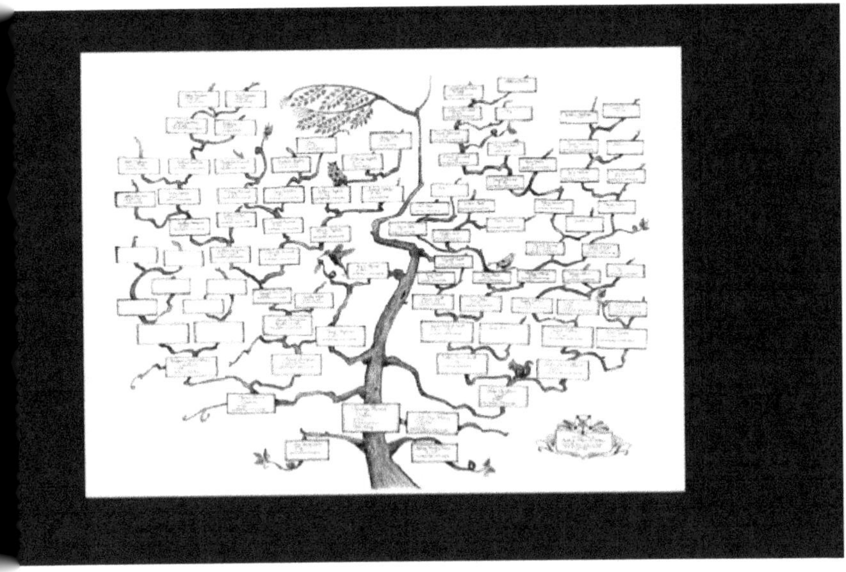

So, one day I was looking through these ancient books that don't exist anymore, and I found this. So, this sign right here I thought it was like, alright, this was a flag that was in the Philippines around the Spanish revolutionary times, said, "Oh, that must stand for "I" independence." But later I found out, no, it was our old writing system, and that's a "K," and that peaked my interest.

Britannica
MICROPÆDIA
Ready
Reference
3
Ceara
Britannica
MICROPÆDIA
Ready
Reference
4
Britannica
MICROPÆDIA
Ready
Reference
5
Britannica
MICROPÆDIA
Ready
Reference
6
Britannica
MICROPÆDIA
Ready
Reference
7
Britannica
MICROPÆDIA
Ready
Reference
8
Britannica
MICROPÆDIA
Ready
Reference
9

I went to this festival, and I saw this man selling books and a calendar, I said, "Hey, that's the letter K, right?" he goes, "Yeah, that's our old writing system," "Well, do you got any more info about it?" "Nah, I don't, sorry." And at that same festival I saw this dance it's called a singkil, and usually when I see dances, cultural dances, they're smiling, trying to entertain, but when I saw this, I was all "Dang, they're like kings and queens, I didn't know that we had that." It was a rediscovery, and that was a similar thing that I heard Brand Nubian and other rap groups talk about, when we were kings, when we were queens, I said, "Oh, I didn't know we had that too," and every single indigenous culture has that, and I just had no idea. The queen was there walking with her head up, she wasn't smiling or dancing for people's other pleasure it was a cultural expression, dude had a sword. That just hit me, and I said, "Alright, this stuff I want to get into."

After I graduated, I went to the Philippines,
meant to stay there for like 6 months,
ended up staying for 10 years.

There I started writing, I use that first symbol that I saw, I started a blog writing about my experience as an American in the country.

KONSHUS PHILIPPINES

This guy actually was my teacher; it's odd. People sometimes go, "Where'd you learn this writing system? Do you have to go to mountains, chop a chicken's head off and do this exotic thing?" I say, "Nah, I learn from a white guy in Canada." (Audience laughter) And that is very typical you don't learn your culture, you're going to have to learn it from someone else which is great, cool guy, never met him but we started corresponding, but that is another lesson.

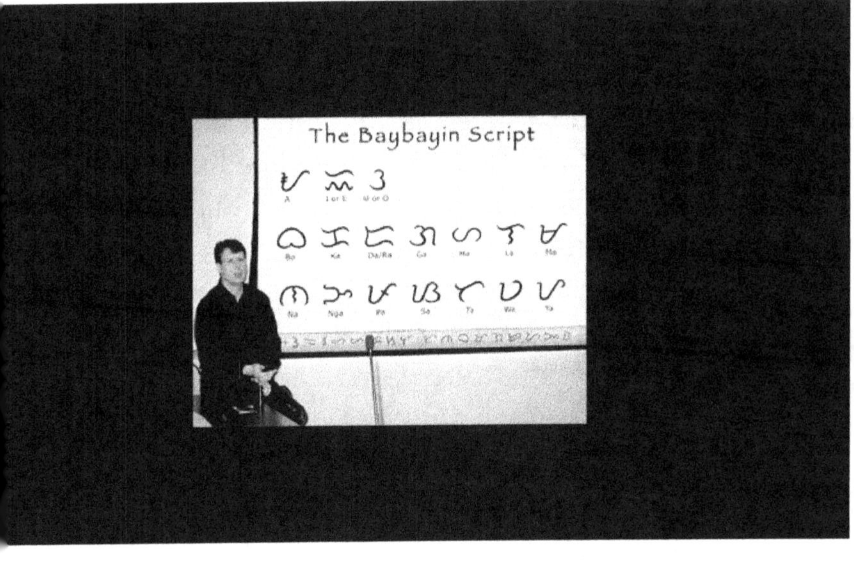
The Baybayin Script

While there I also learned about the indigenous folks, people that are still writing the script. The Aeta tribe, and I thought about my parents and wanted to ask, "Why didn't you ever teach me all this?" My grandparents never taught me about this. I didn't know that we looked like this back then or even today. And that's a thing, and that's that anti-blackness that colonial mentality brings into you. My grandmother would stay out of the sun because she didn't want you to be dark or literally bleach their skin, pinch the nose of the baby. Hopefully, they don't stay like that. I learned about Apo Whang Od, who's the last tattoo practitioner of her generation. She a 100 years old that tattoos.

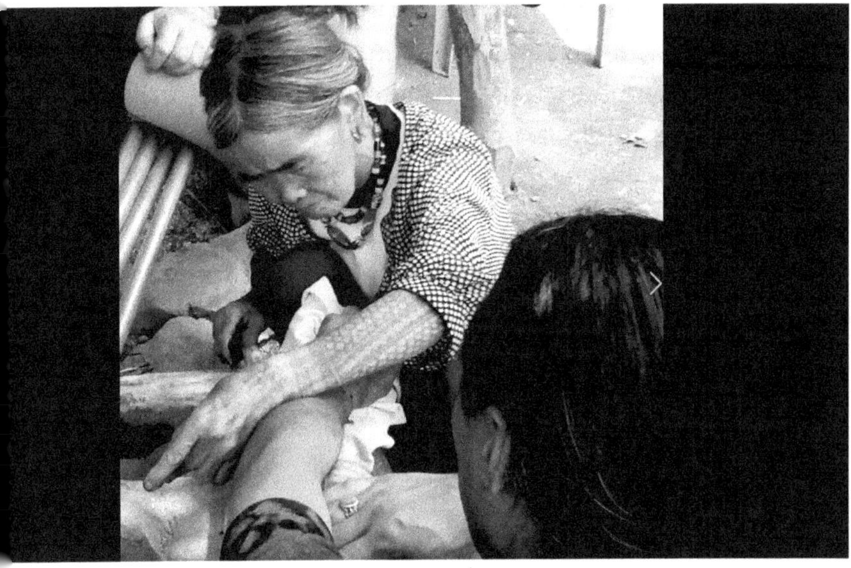

ig@lanewilcken

Living in the Philippines too there was this movement of Hip Hop in the 90's, and literally, there was a war, culture war, Rock Punk versus Hip Hop. And it wasn't just some music battle, there were literally kids that were on the Punk scene, the Rock scene vs. Hip Hop, fighting and stabbing each other in the mall, and I was in the middle of all that. It was really strange.

51

I paid my dues writing this script. My cousins would take me to bars, and I'd write names of people, "Hey, what's your name? Nikki?" And I'll write their name, and then I'll give it to them, that's how I kind of got my practice. But then that showed me that there's social value in practicing culture.

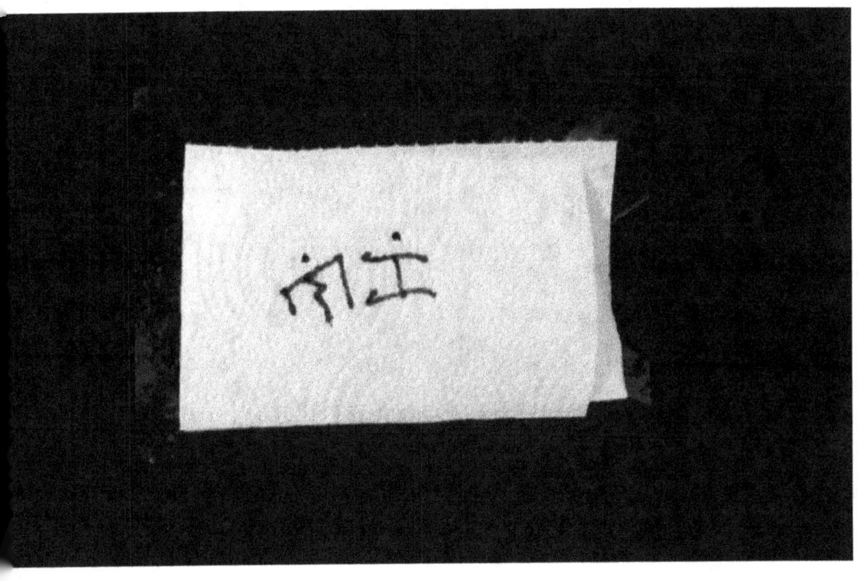

At the time, callcenters were picking up in Manila and since I was an American with an accent, people would tell. Me that I should work at a callcenter and that I could be a manager. I thought I was too good for that so I decided to move back to America with one of my missions to promote Philippine culture I experience and learned.

But when I came back here the only job, I could get was working at a call center. So, I worked at a call center, it sucked; getting yelled at nine hours a day.

But I like anybody that's depressed don't do it, but I did it, got a tattoo. I got a tattoo in the script of my family name, and I thought, "I want to try and promote this."

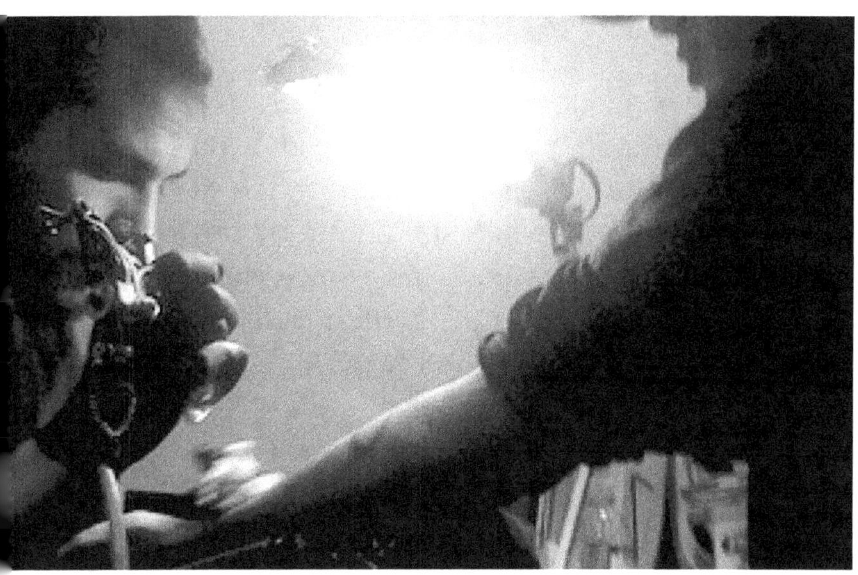

Facebook and all that didn't exist back then, so I taught myself how to make websites. So, I uploaded it on the website, and then people started asking me, "Hey, how do you write this?" They would tell me their stories of their identity like blah, blah, blah and my parents passed away, they never taught me anything. So, through this script is that how that they discovered themselves.

NEWS FEED
COMMENTS
Sign up for email news and updates!
Enter your email address
GO
Blog   Baybayin info   Links   About   FAQ
DOWNLOADS   ERRORS   FEATURED   MODERN   NEWS   STYLES   VIDEOS
I   U   BA   KA   DA   GA   HA   LA
NA   NGA   PA   RA   SA   TA   WA   YA
About
Baybayin aka Alibata is a pre-Filipino writing system from the islands known as the "Philippines". This site is run by Christian Cabuay who also runs PinoyTattoos.com [Read more...]
Search for
SEARCH
Recent Posts
Tags
fonts

That lead to other opportunities like making an app, opening an online school, shooting a doc and then, of course, streetwear, you have your shirts, you have your snapbacks, published some books.

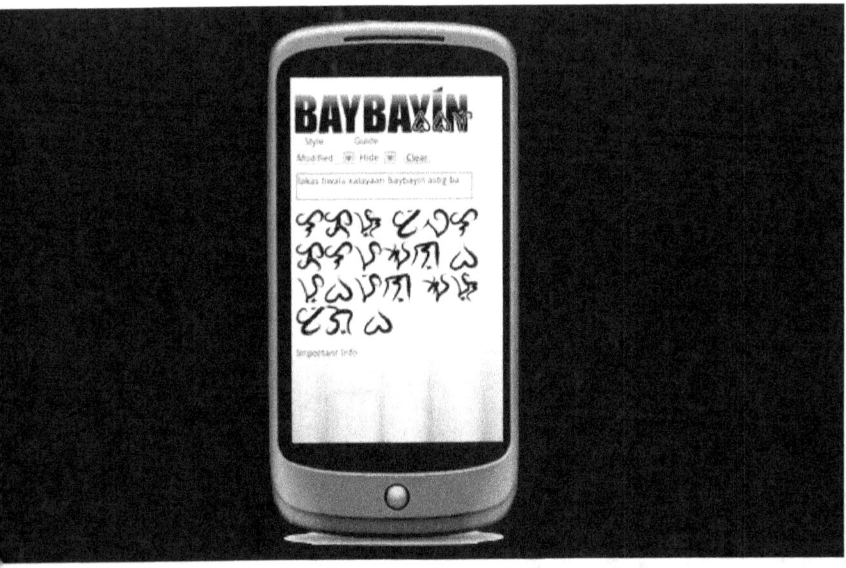
BAYBAYIN
Style
Guide
Modified
Hide
Clear

BAYBAYINSCHOOL

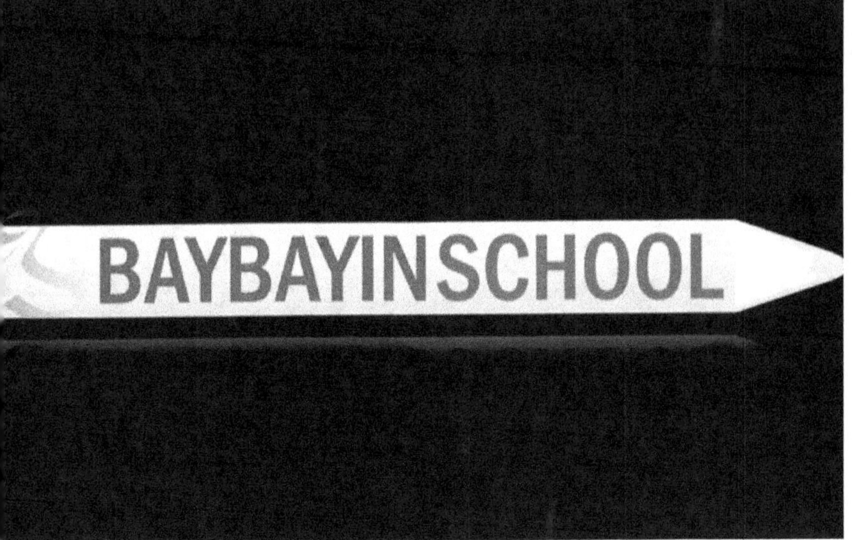

sulat ng malansang isda
a kristian kabuay film

DECOLONIZE
INDIGENIZE

An Introduction to Baybayin
Christian Cabuay

Sulat na Kaluluwa
Writing of the Soul
Art of Kristian Kabuay &
Voices of the Filipino diaspora

FREE Digital Copy
Kulay : Baybayin
PrePhilippine script coloring book
Kristian Kabuay

It gave me more opportunities because I had this side hustle to create more art. With the art I still kept to my graffiti roots.

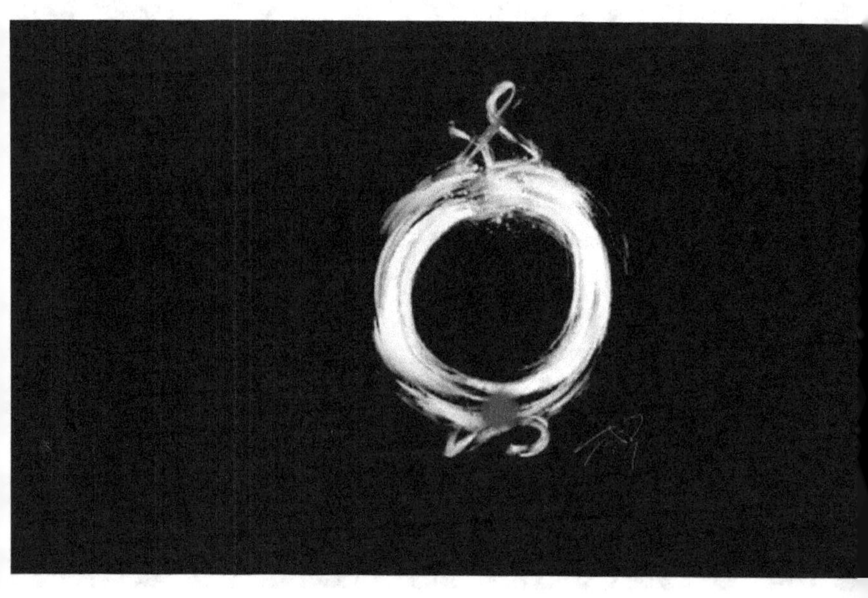

People started asking, "Can you do this live?" "I don't know, I can do it live I guess." Who would want to watch paint dry? That's hella boring. So I started to paint live, doing much bigger pieces.

That eventually lead to doing talks and lectures about it because in this previous screen that I showed you that people would say, "Hey, is that Chinese, is that Japanese?" And again, it brought me back to my childhood like, "What are you?" "Like damn, back again after all this hustle, and I still have to explain." (Audience laughter) So, now I need to speak and give context to the artwork.

filamfest 4h
@baybayin
Workshop
w/ Kristian
@baybayin
UCLA
Our Mission:
Edu
Finding

The way that I like to approach it is identity and expression of that identity.

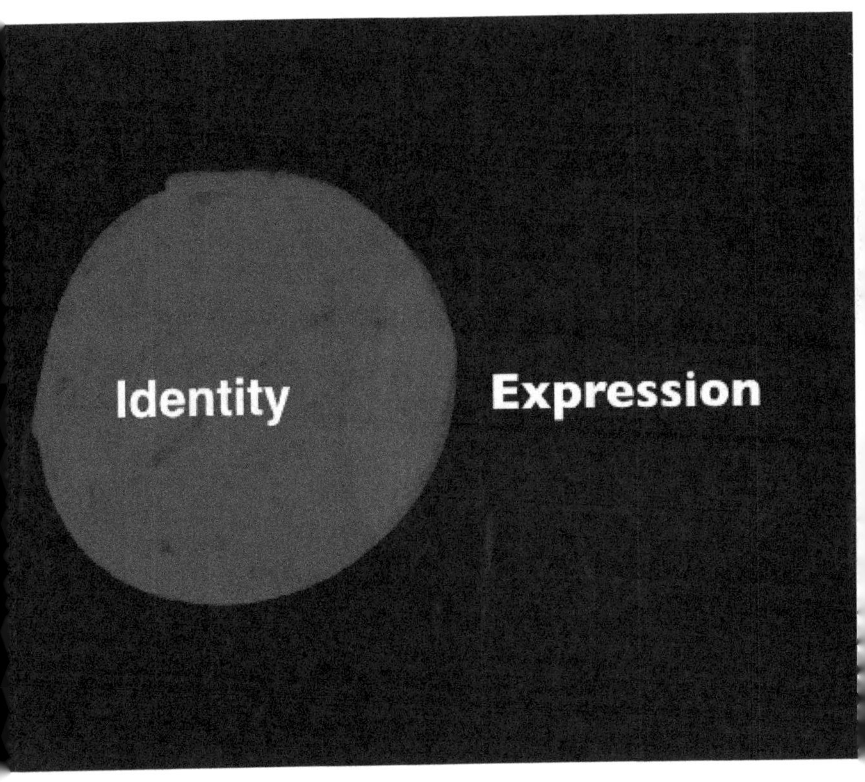
Identity
Expression

The value through Hip Hop: Identity, social and economics. Identity: cultural identity, discovering yourself, knowledge of self. I found that out through KRS One, Public Enemy, Paris, not Paris Hilton, (Audience laughter) Paris from Oakland.

Social, social value: Rock Steady DJs, Kevy Kev KZSU at Stanford, even MC Hammer back in the day.

And then the economics, we all know Russell Simmons the mogul, Marc Echo with the streetwear and Wu-Tang everything from movies, music, the whole nine. With these three value streams of cultural identity, social benefit and economic benefit that is what leads to preservation because if you don't have value, why is something going to be preserved?

Identity

KRS One
Public Enemy
Paris

Social

Rock Steady DJs
Kevy Kev KZSU
MC Hammer

Economics

Russell Simmons
Marc Echo
Wu Tang

I'm going to end this with this with the typical interest sequence within a cultural practice, usually starts off with something cosmetic like you get a tattoo or buy a shirt or buy music then you move into the educational space. Maybe you look up...you go to some lecture, community discussions and maybe become a practitioner of that cultural practice, you write the script, create art, have a business and then advocacy and so, community leadership, activism, writing books.

Typical Interest Sequence

Cosmetic	Educational	Practitioner	Advocate
▸Gets tattoos ▸Buys shirts ▸Buys art	▸Buys books ▸Attends lectures and workshops ▸Participates in discussions	▸Writes the script everyday ▸Creates art ▸Community participation ▸Has a business	▸Community leadership ▸Conducts lectures ▸Runs workshops ▸Writes books ▸Activism

Let's break this down. This side is the consumer side, and the other side is the providers.

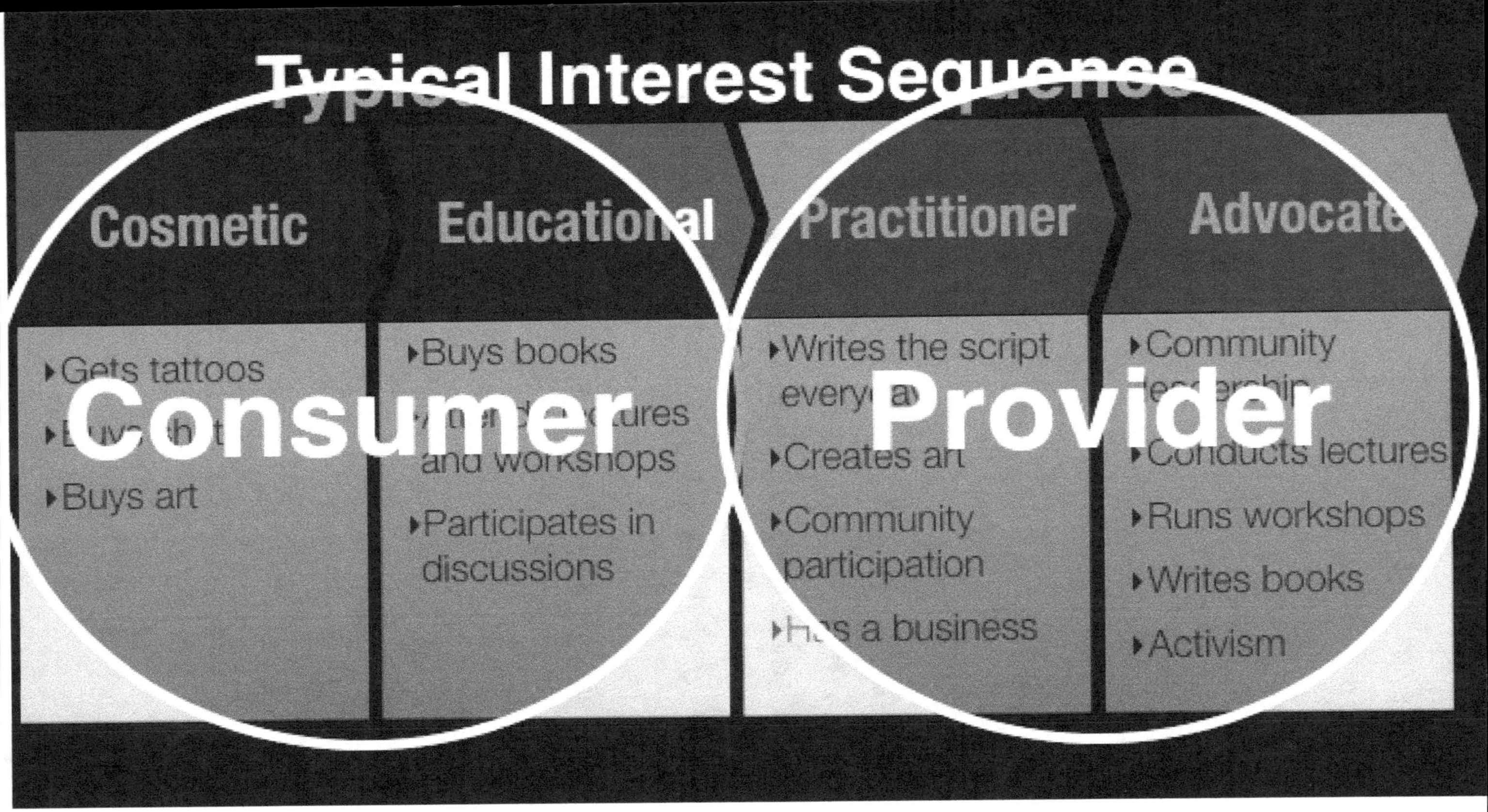

Typical Interest Sequence
Cosmetic
Educational
Practitioner
Advocate
Consumer
Provider
Gets tattoos
Buys art
Buys books
Attends lectures and workshops
Participates in discussions
Writes the script everyday
Creates art
Community participation
Has a business
Community leadership
Conducts lectures
Runs workshops
Writes books
Activism

The job of the practitioners and the advocates is to provide value to those that are within the cosmetics and educational tracks.

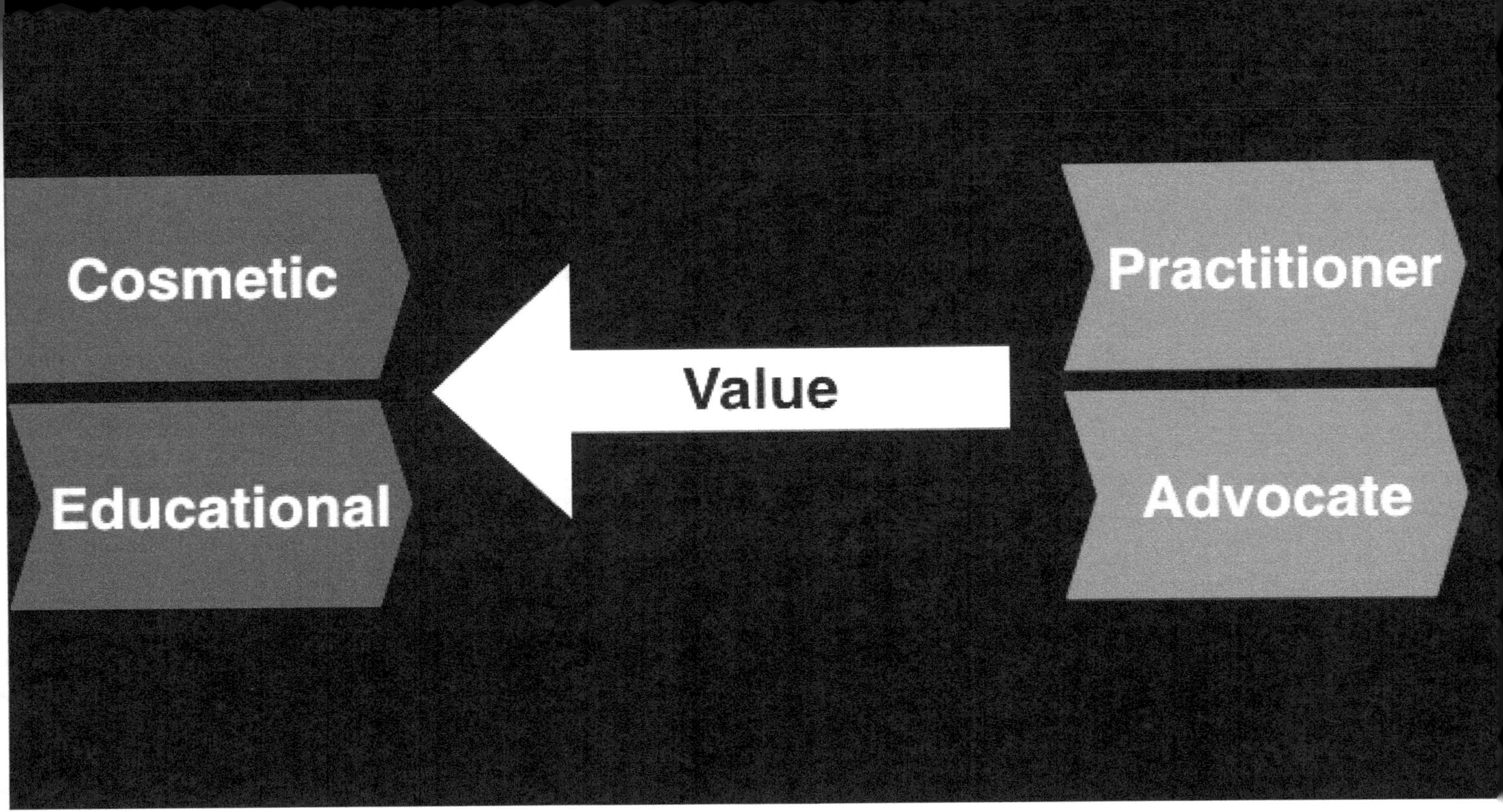

Practitioner
Advocate
Value
Cosmetic
Educational

After talking to a lot of people through my
travels, I learned that it's…

Not about *WRITING* systems

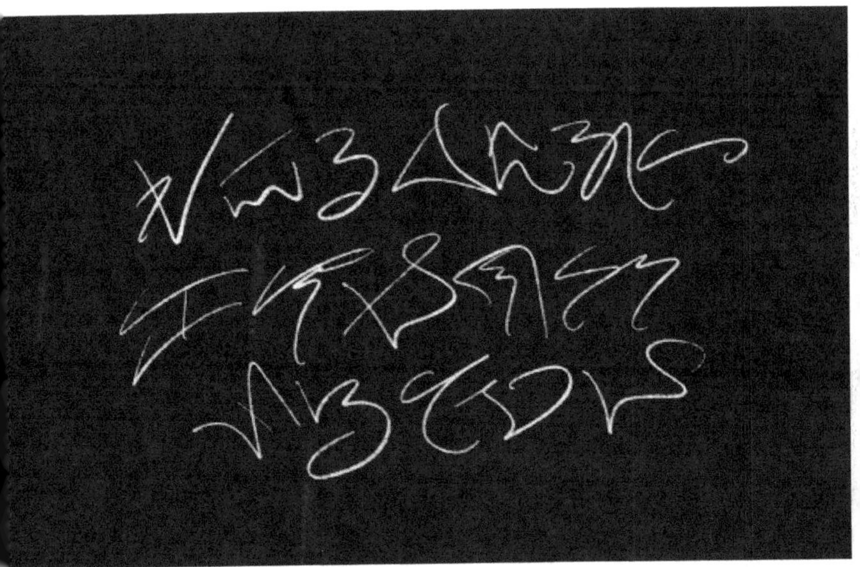

Not about
ART

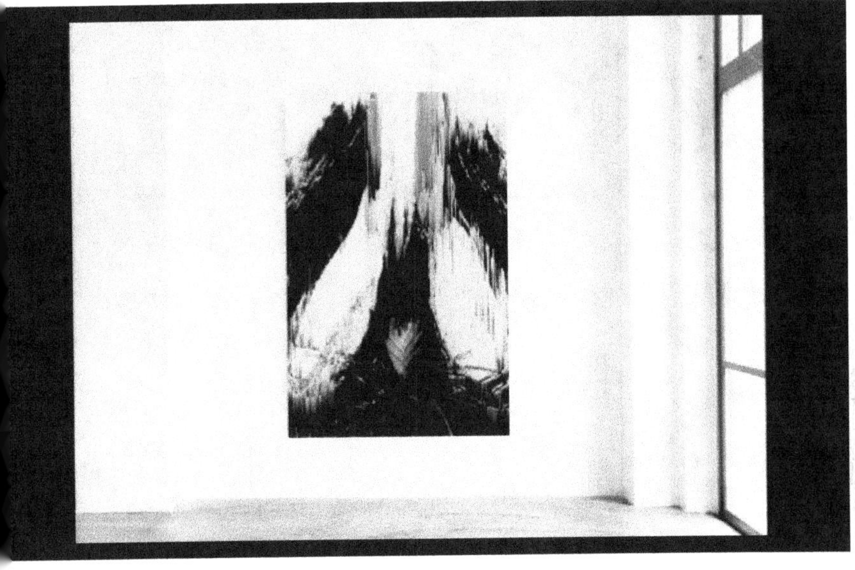

Kristian Kabuay

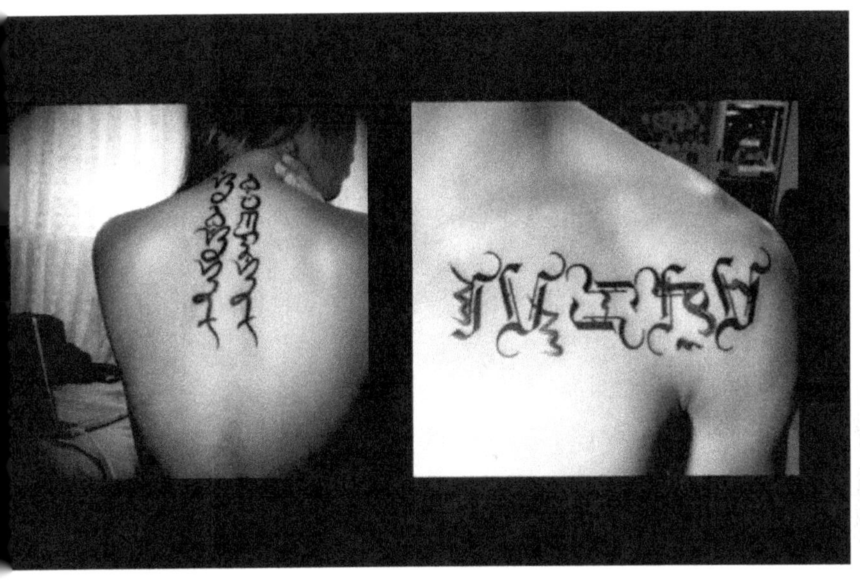

So what's it about?

IDENTITY

Big Daddy Kane has a song that not that many people know of, Who Am I? So, the first verse he was talking about being stolen from Africa then the second he's talking about when he started Hip Hop and then selling out and then the third is actually Malcolm X's daughter, Gamilah Shabazz, and she's talking about aspirations.

Who am I

I was born...A black man from the motherland
Speakin a language today most people don't understan
Where no one could bother me
Cause I had freedom, justice, and equality
But then one day it was tooken away
And I was shipped to the U.S.A

I came out hardcore, flexin cock diesel
Saw a little cash, and pop goes the weasel
I had to make that change and rearrange
My whole rap format, no hardcore rap
So now all the pop charts I rule
Over New Kids on the Block and Paula Abdul, huh
I thought I made it, then my song faded
And none of the black stations ever have played it
I tried to blame it on MTV
And say, "Damn, they cold played me for Young MC"

Like the women of long ago, I am also here
Also to show, I have the courage
Have the strength, I'm for equal opportunity

There's an old saying in my country - Ang hindi mamahal sa sariling wika, daig pa sa hayop at malansang isda. In English that translates to "For those that don't love their own language or culture is worse than an animal and a stinky fish." So don't be a stinky fish

Salamat - Thank you
(Audience applause)

Rediscovering an Ancient Script Through Hip Hop

Surat Kamay collection

Kristian Kabuay
kabuay.com

Filp-One
flip1sba.com

RJ Sison
ig@pamanadesigns

Ray Haguisan
ig@kapuwaco

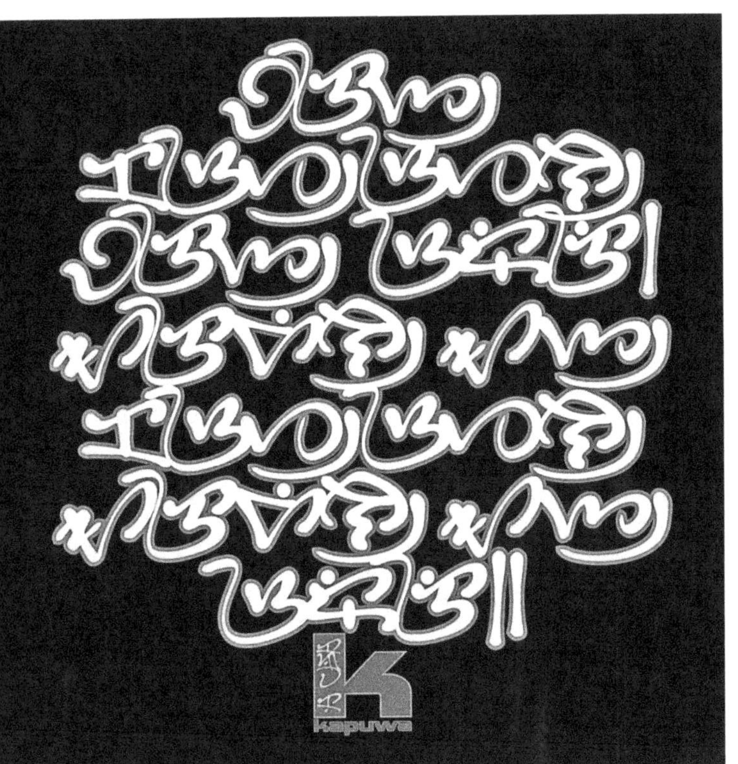

Bayani Art
bayaniart.com

Sami See
samisee.com

Nate Gayatinea
ig@natestomp900

Ang Gerilya
ig@anggerilya

~~Hustle Hard~~
Hustle Smart

Rediscovering an Ancient Script Through Hip Hop

Kristian Kabuay

ISBN: 9781720015079

Design, transcription, and writing were done as a
Labor Day weekend project from September 1-3, 2018

kabuay.com
ig @baybayin
fb/kristiankabuay
k@kabuay.com